The Sun Will Shine Again

Kaitlyn Walsh

BookLeaf
Publishing

India | USA | UK

Presentation by *BookLeaf Publishing*

Web: www.bookleafpub.com

E-mail: info@bookleafpub.com

ISBN: 9789363311589

First edition 2024

*This book is (unapologetically extensively)
dedicated to:*

My Jesus ~ I owe everything to Him.

My family;

*My parents ~ I wouldn't be who I am today
without you. I love you beyond words.*

*My siblings and sister-in-law ~ You all mean
the world to me.*

*My nephew Liam, and niece Eleanore ~ I pray
that when you get bigger, and face hard things,
you'll always cling to God... and know your
Auntie loves you!*

*My grandparents; Grammy, Grandpa &
Grandma Newton, Grandpa & Grandma Walsh
~ I love you all very much.*

*My 'unbiological grandparents' Grandma &
Grandpa Supiran ~ Thank you for being a
prime example of walking through trials with
grace and faith.*

My dear God-given friends;

Ryanne ~ thank you for always being there for me, even in my darkest times, being my iron friend.

Makynna ~ thank you for walking with me through the trials of life, and always pointing me back to Christ.

Lauren ~ so thankful to have you as my friend for 10 years, thank you for brightening my days. On the hard days, remember, the sun will shine again.

Lindsey, Jenna ~ thank you for being my sweet, thoughtful friends, refreshing my soul all the time! (Proverbs 27:9)

The Davidsons ~ my second parents & family, loving friends, and comedic comrades. Love you all!

Some of my spiritual mentors;

Alissa, Katie and Mark, Kylie, Missi and Jason ~ thank you for investing in my life, and always guiding me to Christ.

Victoria ~ you've blessed me with constant encouragement in every hardship, for as long as I can remember. Thank you.

My physical therapist, family friend, encourager, listener ~ Jen, thank you for going above and beyond your job, and impacting my life through this journey.

My sweet bosses ~ Vic & Linda, thank you for loving me, and reminding me to be somebody's sunshine. ;)

Lastly,

To every person who has walked through, is walking through, or will soon walk through a painful trial. Stay strong. Trust God. The sun will shine again.

ACKNOWLEDGEMENT

Thank you to BookLeaf Publishing for making it possible for me to achieve this dream.

Thank you to my mom and my dad for supporting me in my every endeavor, being my biggest fans, sticking by my side in the hard times, and endlessly providing for me and helping me to achieve my goals. Mama and Poppy, I could never do it without you.

And most of all, I praise the Lord for His provision and blessing. For the gift He's given me, and the opportunity He's given me to use it. For every hard journey He's allowed me to walk through, that has brought me to a deeper knowledge of His grace and His faithfulness, and that has refined and strengthened me. Without Him, I am nothing. All glory be to Him.

PREFACE

Everyone knows hard times. I was inspired to write poetry as a result of walking through a difficult trial in my life. In less than one year, my life was turned upside down by hardships - I went through two major hip surgeries and hard recoveries less than a year apart, and lost someone very dear to me during the same time. Writing helped me process and cope, but greater than that, I leaned hard on God, and had the privilege of seeing Him carry me through my darkest of days.

Reality is, hardships are going to come. There are some tough trials in this life. But the sweet truth is that we are never alone. God has a purpose and a plan. He brings beauty from ashes. You will make it through, and you'll be stronger for it.

So on the days when the pain is extra deep, hope feels farther than ever, when life is weighing heavy... remember, even in your darkest moments, the sun will shine again.

A Sunrise of Hope

There are days that feel like darkness,
Overshadowed by this life's great sorrow,
But on those days, there is yet hope
For the sun will still rise tomorrow.

You may feel you won't make it,
The day is too painful and long
But hold on through the night,
A sunrise of hope will shine at dawn.

The pain won't last forever,
In the morning joy will come,
Even when nothing else seems right,
You can be sure to see the rising sun.

God pours color to the sky to give you hope,
To remind you of His daily mercies anew.
For after every single tear-filled night,
He paints a sunrise in the sky for you.

So when this life starts looking down,
Choose to lift your eyes!
When hope feels far, remember this:
The sun will still always rise.

Too Hard

This is just too much for me,
I'm running out of air.
I feel like I can hardly breathe,
This just feels so unfair.

I'm trying not to think this way,
Wondering why it has to be me.
I know it will all make sense one day,
But that day is hard to see.

I don't want to do this anymore,
I'm so tired of pushing through.
Perhaps this is what I was created for,
But it's the hardest thing I've ever had to do.

No light at the end of the tunnel, it feels
Each painful step to get nowhere,
Trying to trust whatever God wills,
But my heart aches, waiting to get there.

I'm trying so hard to look at this right,
But hope feels far out of reach.
Walking by faith, not by sight
I want to learn what God has to teach.

I'm trying, but it's hard.
I feel like I'm drowning each day,
Can't keep my head above water
But there is no other way.

For some reason, that is beyond me
God chose for me this pain.
I'm trying my best always to be
A testimony for His name.

This is good, though hard to see how,
I know that I'll live to tell the story.
I must patiently endure for now,
But it will be worth it all, for His glory.

Suffering Now

One day, there's peace
The next, there's pain.
Walking right through sunshine
Into a season of heavy rain.

Suffering and grief,
Loss staring you in the face,
Until you find yourself on your knees,
Begging God for His amazing grace.

This life brings many sorrows,
More pain than you feel you can bear,
The weight of the world on your shoulders,
Your hardships feel anything but fair.

But reach out your hand,
And let hope fall into your grasp.
Because there is for you prepared
Something far more than you could think or ask.

Suffering now is nothing,
When compared to your eternal glory.
To suffer here is simply one page
Written in a never-ending, beautiful story.

To suffer now will be glory then.
To feel a fraction of the pain Jesus went through,
To go through trials, and someday learn
That there is so much beauty waiting for you.

The suffering is not worthy of comparison to the
glory.
All the pain dims in Christ's magnificent light,
To feel pain now, yet keep the faith,
How amazing to hear God say, "Well done.
You have fought the good fight."

Tired

I am tired of feeling I must be okay,
Tired of hiding the tears in my eyes.
I'm tired of putting a smile on everyday,
I'm tired of living a perfect life of lies.
I'm tired.
Tired of pretending to be what everyone needs;
"The one who has it all together", isn't that me?
I'm "the perfectionist who always succeeds",
I can't fail, that's not who I'm supposed to be.
I'm tired.
Tired of always putting on a façade,
Just to hide that my life is a mess too.
Try to keep my problems between me and God,
I act like everything's fine, but it's just not true.
I'm tired.
Tired of trying and still falling apart,
I'm too scared to be completely real.
What if someone sees into my reticent heart?
Can't let them find out the things that I feel.
I'm tired.
It's exhausting, pretending to be
Just "the one who has it all together" all the
time;
Try though I might, that just isn't me,
I'm not the perfect Christian who's always fine...
I'm tired.

Keep Fighting

Hi.
I'm talking to you -
The one who currently feels like they can't keep
pushing through.
I'm talking to the one whose heart is broken in a
million pieces,
The one being told to keep going, but who can't
find any reasons.
I'm talking to the one wondering if there's any
point anymore,
I'm talking to you -
the one who feels there's nothing worth living
for.
The one who thinks they're just out there, taking
up space,
The one who feels they don't belong, they don't
have a place.
I'm talking to the one who's sad and doesn't even
know why,
The one who doesn't have any tears left in them
to cry,
And the one who's quietly sobbing, and feels
they have to hide,
The one who's fought with everything in them to
look fine on the outside...

Hi there.
I'm talking to you.
I'm so proud of you for all you have fought
through.
I just want to let you know that you are seen,
You're doing amazing, I know life can get pretty
mean.
I know you've heard it before,
And it feels pointless to hear it once more,
But please,
Please keep fighting.
Just wait until the cloud passes and you see
things in better lighting.
Don't give up now, please.
If you're too weak to stand, fall to your knees.
Whatever you do, just do not quit!
God's not finished with you, I'm absolutely sure
of it.
Your heart is still beating, your lungs are still
breathing,
God woke you up today for a reason!
Hang in there, hope is not gone,
God has plans for you, and they're not yet done.
I'm talking to you -
the one hurting inside;
The one for whom Jesus willingly died.
He died to give you life each day,
Please, I beg you, don't throw that away.
It gets better, I promise it's true.

And if you find that hard to believe...
Then I wrote this
for you.

Praise in the Pain

It's hard to see now,
The purpose in my pain.
It's hard to see how
I can dance in the rain.

I can wince and I can cry,
It hurts too much to bear,
But after a teardrop and a sigh,
A hard-fought smile I can wear.

Because I know that I am weak,
But I have a strong God!
In pain, I can barely speak,
But He has heard me all along.

In worship, I can lift my heart,
When my body can barely move.
My soul rejoices in who You are,
Even as it cries in pain to You.

I'm so tired and so worn,
But I'm learning to dance in the rain.
Seeking Your face amidst the storm,
Lord, teach me to praise You in the pain.

In the Valley

I'm walking through a valley right now,
Mountains behind and ahead -
Things I have gotten through,
And mountains I haven't fully climbed yet.

I learned a lot from the past mountains,
Left a lot of pain behind.
Now I'm standing in a valley,
Looking at a mountain yet to be climbed.

I remember the last mount,
Standing victoriously on the peak,
Looking at where I had come from,
And how God carried me when I was weak.

I have grown since then,
I'm stronger than I was yesterday.
And by God's grace, I'll climb again,
And trust that He will make a way.

It's hard, walking here,
Through this valley of pain,
Seeing another mountain ahead,
And dark clouds full of rain.

But I will walk.
Each day, one step at a time.
For I know my God holds my hand,
Through the valley, and the climb.

Rain or Shine

I think we glorify
dancing in the rain sometimes...
And we forget to dance
on days when the sun shines.
We put so much emphasis
on rejoicing when life is hard,
We forget sometimes
to enjoy life wherever we are.
I'm not saying it's bad to rejoice
while in a season of pain,
I just believe, we too often forget to thank God
when we're not walking through rain.
We get so used to living a life
of comfort and ease,
That we only realize how blessed we've been
when a trial brings us to our knees!
When someone goes through a hard time,
we praise them for having a good attitude,
But when life is good and nothing's wrong,
we neglect to live a life of gratitude.
The mountaintops are so much sweeter
after having endured the climb,
But we so quickly forget the wonder
of seeing that breathtaking view for the first
time.

Life is made up of many sentences of blessing,
merely punctuated with moments of pain,
Yet too often, we forget
that how we spend our days of sunshine,
is just as important as
dancing in the rain.

Ok to not be Ok

I've been told
That it's okay... to not be okay.
They say it so easily,
Make it sound so cliché.

"It's okay to not be okay!"
But, for how long?
How many days after the heartbreak
Does not being fine become wrong?

I don't know...
I guess grief doesn't have an expiration date,
And I'm not there yet,
But I'm sure healing is worth the wait.

But I wonder,
Why is it okay to not be okay?
Who decided
That I'm allowed to be sad today?

It's okay...
Because we're only human, I suppose.
We don't reach perfection,
We only reach growth.

And God knows.
He knows that sometimes we have bad days,
He knows this life brings pain,
And He covers it with His amazing grace.

I am not okay right now.
But, I am still blessed.
All I can do is be content where I'm at,
And trust God with the rest.

Talking with God

Hey God,
It's me.
Once again.
I'm so prone to complain, to cry, to question.
Always asking for hep,
And rarely stopping to just worship and praise.
And I'm sorry, God, but that's where I am right
now,
and where I've been for days.
In desperate need of Your strength and healing,
Begging for Your gracious help.
I know that I said "Lord-willing",
But it's been harder than I imagined, and I really
need You now.
I need You always, but especially at this time,
Because there are moments I feel so weak,
and I can't get the pain out of my mind.
I know Your truth, I know all the things there are
to know.
And I also know You understand,
You will hold me up, and won't ever let go.

Changing Seasons

One day, everything feels perfectly right...
The next, you're crying into your pillow at night.
It's confusing and uncertain, but that's just how
life goes.
Sometimes the answer to our "why?", only God
knows.
We may never know what the purpose is for our
pain,
But you know, flowers only grow after they've
endured rain.
But don't forget, of course, they need sunshine
too!
So even when it's bleak, know that the sun will
eventually shine through.
And we may never know God's answer to our
heartbroken "why?"
But we do know His plans for us are good, and
His ways are high.
That's the thing about living this life, that we
must know -
God has declared promises to us, and when He
says it,
it is so.
The promises He's given are unchanging and
true,

And we must learn that when life gets hard,
He's always there for us to turn to.

Yet I will Worship

The Lord gives, and He takes away.
And I will choose to bless His name either way.
In the beauty, or in the ash and pain,
May my heart always choose to bless His name.
I want to be in a state of worship all the time.
I want to rejoice in the very fact that Jesus is
mine!
I will praise, even in the hardest and most
painful thing,
He's put a new song in my mouth, and I will
sing.
The Lord is my shepherd, and He takes good
care of me,
For that reason, louder than the hurt will my
worship be.
When I look up and see storm clouds and rain,
In the storm of life, I will bless His name.
When my world feels to be caving in,
Even as it crumbles... Yet I will worship Him.
When the hurt is very deep, and I'm running out
of air,
I will take my burdens to His throne, and leave
them there.
Even when it's hard, I will choose to praise,

Because my Lord has never forsaken me, all of
my days.
Good and bad - He stays just the same,
And in sickness or health, I will bless His name.
He protects me, guides me, and loves me so
fully,
I don't deserve to be in the presence of a God so
holy.
But He is faithfully there for me, always.
And forever he is worthy of my praise.
So even with a broken heart,
Even as I feel I'm falling apart,
And even if it feels I always will...
Yet I will worship still.

Level One

Sometimes, you have to start back at level one.
And it's not because you haven't worked hard
enough,
In fact, often it's to teach you how much you can
overcome -
Obstacles stacked high, that you've risen above.

It may feel like you're taking two steps forward,
and one step back.
But later you will see what every step was
purposed for.
Sometimes we have to work harder to get past a
setback,
And that's when we realize we're capable of so
much more.

Maybe you're taking baby steps,
Maybe progress feels long and slow,
But baby steps are steps nonetheless,
And if you just keep taking them, you'll be
surprised at how far you'll go.

Sometimes we face hardship so we can be a
light,
By the effort we put in, how we live each day.

It's not easy, and we won't always get it right,
But our weakness is Christ's power on display.

Grace upon grace, poured over our lives,
He gives us new strength untainted.
One day, on eagles' wings we will rise,
Walking roads on which we once fainted.

So if you find yourself at level one, feeling low...
Stay humble, work hard, God will lift you high.
Don't you dare give up hope,
Remember, there is always a reason why.

Would I do it Again?

I was asked if I would do it again -
This trial I've been walking through.
Would I go through it again?
Even though it was by far the hardest thing I've
ever had to do?
My answer was
yes.
And I know that "in a heartbeat" sounds really
cliché...
But, in a heartbeat, I would walk through this
again,
Simply to watch God carry me again through
every single day.
Would I really go through it again?
Yes.
One hundred percent.
Because although I know the pain,
I also know there was a purpose for every hard
place I went.
Even though it was so difficult,
Knowing that, would I do it again?
Yes, I would.
Because I've never drawn closer to the Lord than
I did then.
I've grown, I've learned;

I'm not at all the same girl I was before,
And though it took a lot of pain to get here,
What I have gained is worth a whole lot more.
If I did have to go through it again,
It would be a struggle, I know.
But if God wanted me to walk that road,
Then there is nowhere else I'd rather go.
I am thankful God entrusted this trial to me,
I'm thankful for the bad days, as well as the good.
And if God asked me to do it again...
Yes.
I really would.

Stronger

They say
"what doesn't kill you, makes you stronger"
And I know the Lord renews my strength,
But I don't want to wait any longer.

Yet it's in the waiting
That I always see God come through.
It's in the stillness
That I realize there's nothing better I could do.

Nothing better than to just trust,
To just patiently wait.
And the Lord will make me stronger,
In His perfect time; He never runs late.

God's put me through the Refiner's Fire,
Because He wants to refine, reshape, and
remold.
It's hot, and it hurts,
But when I've been tried, I will come forth as
gold.

I will survive this heartache,
And I will be stronger for it.
The Lord promises His abundant grace,
And now I beg Him to pour it.

I must remember
He has a purpose for the pain.
He will bring beauty from the ash,
I will see the sun again, after the rain.

My strength lies not in myself,
But in the God of all grace.
His strength is perfected in my weakness,
I find joy in the light of His face.

It is He who makes me stronger,
It is He who carries me through the hardest
night.
It is by His grace I've come this far,
And by His grace I've fought this fight.

He has a plan for this hardship,
A purpose for every tear I have cried.
And I will be stronger than ever,
When I reach the other side.

In the Stillness

Lord,
I need to hear Your voice,
My mind is so cluttered, filled with noise.
I search for You in the wind and the hurricane,
But instead, I always hear the pouring rain.
I seek You in the tornado, but You're nowhere to
be found,
I listen in the fire, but I cannot hear a sound.
Lord, I need to hear You speak,
My heart is weary, my faith is weak.
Please God, deafen my ears to all other noise,
And let me hear only
Your soft, still voice.

"Just Tired"

"I'm just tired."
This can be interpreted in many different ways -
Sometimes it honestly refers to lack of sleep,
But often, it's more than just physically tired
phase.

It can be an exhaustion much deeper,
Complete emotional fatigue,
An exhaustion that says
"I can't do this! I'm just too weak."

"I'm tired."
But not from a lack of sleep,
I'm tired...
Because life right now is draining me
emotionally.

I'm about ready to give up,
My effort is taking such a toll.
I don't know what to do anymore,
But it's been so long since I've felt whole.

I'm truly exhausted, but
I'll keep going - I need to.
This life is still a gift,
And God still has a work for me to do.

I can't give up, though I want to.
I can't. Not now.
Because I will eventually make it through,
Someday. Somehow.

Heart of the Doctor

I keep finding myself feeling broken,
Even though I have really been trying.
I've been trying to be okay and move past this,
But I guess my smile has sometimes been lying.
Because the truth is, I'm not.
I don't know when I will ever be.
And I want so bad to be perfect,
So I put on this dishonest, pretend,
composed, impression of me.
I tell myself I'm getting better,
Because I think that I should be by now.
And I tell myself that it's time for life to move
on,
But I still helplessly lay here, wondering how.
I talk to God, and tell Him His will is all that I
want to do.
I really do.
But sometimes I say the words,
and it's so hard to actually follow through.
And I lay here, at war in my heart,
And I feel guilty for falling apart.
I feel guilty for not being better,
I feel guilty for not feeling peace,
Because I truly want to surrender

But I don't even have the strength to get down
on my knees.
I don't have the strength to do it,
I don't have the words to pray.
And the perfectionist within me wants to get it
all right,
So I search for the words I think God wants to
hear me say.
And I forget
that a doctor doesn't come to heal the healthy,
but the ill.
And Jesus came, knowing I'd be empty -
He expects me to have a cup that I need him to
fill.
He has never once expected perfection of me,
Not once has He said that broken was something
I'm not allowed to be.
He came to heal the sick, help the poor, and seek
the lost,
If I could ever be perfect,
He wouldn't have had to endure the cross.
But He did. Because I can't.
And I don't have to try to be something that I'm
not.
He's the hero in this story,
Why should I diminish the pain He already
fought?
I am not perfect. And this side of heaven,
I simply never will be.

So I can come to Jesus broken, just as I am.
For that is all He has ever wanted of me.

Not our Home

If you're wondering why life is hard,
Why it feels like the world is against you,
It's because we're not meant to feel at home here
-
We're just strangers passing through.

Life is hard, because it is flawed,
We live in a broken world today.
We aren't supposed to feel comfortable here,
Because this world is not where we're meant to
stay.

If life was perfect here,
The hope of eternity wouldn't mean a thing.
It's the hopeful expectation of a better place,
That far surpasses any pleasure this world can
bring.

If we were comfortable here,
Well, we'd have no desire to leave!
We'd have nothing to look forward to,
We'd never know joy if didn't first know grief.

This world is not our home.
One day, we'll understand the insignificance of
this place,
Because one day, we'll experience the absolute
joy
Of seeing Jesus, face to face.

Foot of the Cross

When I haven't the strength even to stand,
I will kneel; I will kneel at the cross.
On my knees, Jesus, I lift my hands,
Here I cry, at the foot of the cross.

Help me, Lord, hear my cry.
Hold me, Lord, give me hope!
Your grace to me do not deny,
Carry me, when I can hardly cope.

God, You are faithful and just,
You've never failed, You never will.
When I'm afraid, in You I will trust,
In the storm, You whisper, "Peace, be still."

I'm hurting, Lord, I don't understand.
This burden, too heavy for me to bear.
Help me, Lord, please hold my hand,
And I will follow You, no matter where...

Through the valley, across stormy seas,
Down the painful road of loss.
Wherever it is, find me on my knees,
Forever I will kneel at the foot of the cross.

The Sun will Shine Again

The storm is raging,
Clouds cover the sky.
Your heart is breaking,
There are no tears left in you to cry.

It hurts.

The pain is so deep.
Stuck in a valley,
The mountain ahead looks far too steep.
You wander in this shadow land
Searching for any light,
Even a tiny spark of hope
Might push you to keep up the fight.

It's hard.

Walking this road of pain.
You search for a glimpse of the sun,
But all around is pouring rain.
Just when the darkness closes in
You hear a voice in the dead of night
"Do not be afraid, child,
You will soon find the light."
He takes your hand in His,

Step by step, He gently leads you.
Suddenly you find strength,
When you thought you'd never make it through.
The darkness is long and painful,
But He finally says, "Look up, my child. Don't
you see?
The sun will always shine again,
Just keep on trusting me."